Unlocking Your Great Potential Within You

The Supernatural Powers of Meditation, Executive Functioning Skills, and Good Habits A Guide for Raising Purposeful and Powerful Digital Citizens

Alisa L. Grace

Unlocking Your Great Potential Within You

The Supernatural Powers of Meditation, Executive Functioning Skills, and Good Habits

A Guide for Raising Purposeful and Powerful Digital Citizens

Alisa L. Grace

Self-Published by
Alisa L. Grace
Sanford, FL 32771

ISBN: 978-1-966129-80-6

First Edition
Printed in the United States of America
Library of Congress Cataloging-in-Publication Data

Grace, Alisa L.

Title of the Book: Unlocking Your Great Potential Within You: The Supernatural Powers of Meditation, Executive Functioning Skills, and Good Habits. A Guide for Raising Purposeful and Powerful Digital Citizens

Disclaimer: The views expressed in this book are those of the author and do not necessarily reflect any organizations or individuals mentioned.

Acknowledgments: The author wishes to thank God, Her Husband (Linion), Victory Temple of God, Florida SPECS, Unity Youth Association, All About Serving You, Angels-ANJ Events, NordeVest, and Love & Create Life for their support and contributions.

♥ DEDICATION PAGE

To Parents:

You are your child's first teacher, their daily example, and the constant prayer warrior behind every breakthrough. This book honors your strength, your struggle, and your desire to raise children who thrive in both the digital world and the real one. May these pages bring you hope, strategy, and peace.

To Teachers & Program Leaders:

You carry the sacred responsibility of preparing this generation for a future we cannot yet see. You are not simply instructing minds—you are unlocking hearts, shaping habits, and modeling leadership. This guide was written with you in mind: practical tools in one hand, divine purpose in the other.

To the Students:

You are not defined by a screen. You are not just followers—you are leaders. You have power, wisdom, and purpose already inside you. This journey is about discovering who you truly are… and how to use your phone to reflect that greatness.

📖 A Note to the Reader

This book was designed to be more than just a resource—it is a **companion guide** to the full curriculum, *Unlocking Your Great Potential Within You: The Supernatural Powers of Meditation, Executive Functioning Skills, and Good Habits*, written specifically for children and youth ages **3 through the teenage years**.

Whether you're a parent, teacher, summer learning program leader, or faith-based mentor, this guide works hand-in-hand with the original curriculum to help you implement its core principles—**meditation, executive functioning skills, and good habits**—with **purposeful digital strategies** that promote growth in every environment:

- ✓ At home
- ✓ In the classroom
- ✓ During summer programs
- ✓ And within the community

This companion book provides:

- Practical lesson integrations and activities from all 11 curriculum chapters
- Digital tool suggestions and app usage with intention and wisdom
- Real-life examples for each age group

- Guided reflections and sample agreements
- A full digital citizenship training framework
- And supportive coaching for adults leading the next generation

If you already own the curriculum, this guide will deepen your ability to bring it to life in today's digital world.

If you're discovering this book first, it can serve as a launching point to explore the full **Unlocking Your Great Potential Within You** program for children ages 3–Teen.

Thank you for choosing to lead with faith, structure, and compassion. You are not just managing devices—you are mentoring destinies.

Let's unlock greatness—together.

📖 Table of Contents

✦ Introduction: Reimagining Technology as a Tool for Transformation

We are raising the most connected generation in human history—yet one of the most emotionally distracted. Technology has become the third parent, the substitute teacher, the silent voice shaping our children's attention, values, and identity.

But this isn't a book about banning phones. This is a book about **training**.

We believe technology can be:

- A mirror of identity
- A notebook of dreams
- A tracking device for growth
- A digital journal of the supernatural power within

This guide is grounded in the foundational message of the **Unlocking Your Great Potential Within You** curriculum—where children are taught that they possess **supernatural powers** of:

- Meditation (inner calm and God connection)
- Executive Functioning (clear thinking and wise action)
- Good Habits (consistency and character)

Our mission is to show **parents and educators** how to **train children to use their phones with the same intention** as we teach them to pray, plan, think, and live.

✉ A Letter to Parents: Training, Not Locking

Dear Parent,

You are the gatekeeper of your child's development. Whether your child is 3 or 13, your posture around phone use teaches them how to relate to the most powerful tool they will ever carry.

Too often, we hide phones in fear, use them as pacifiers, or remove them in frustration. But what if we used them to **build connection, calm, and character**?

This guide does not recommend unlimited use but **purposeful** and **parent-directed use**.

Together, we'll explore how you can:

- Model phone use that reflects spiritual and emotional maturity
- Teach your child to use phones for goal setting, gratitude, and meditation.
- Create boundaries that build **trust**, not fear.

The goal is not control. The goal is **self-leadership**.

With you in every step,

— *A Fellow Grand Parent in the Digital Fight*

💼 A Letter to Teachers & Program Leaders: Discipleship Through Devices

Dear Educator, Facilitator, and Coach,

You stand at the intersection of formation and future.

Phones are part of your classroom. But so is transformation.

You are uniquely positioned to show students that their phones are not just entertainment machines—they can be planning tools, creativity stations, reflection journals, and meditation centers.

This guide helps you:

- Incorporate purposeful phone use into every chapter of your learning program
- Use technology to support executive functioning, good habits, and spiritual awareness.
- Shift the student mindset from "consumer" to **creator**, from "follower" to **leader.**

We need digital discipleship now more than ever. You are the leader who will make it real.

With admiration and support,

— *Your Partner in Purposeful Teaching*

📖 Chapter 1:
The Dangers of Untrained Tech Use

Why this guide is more than a suggestion—it's a necessity

"If we do not train our children to use technology wisely, technology will train them without wisdom."

Overview

Technology is neutral. Its power lies in how it is **used**, **understood**, and **integrated** into a child's life. When we fail to intentionally train children in how to use phones and devices, we don't simply "pause" their development—we expose them to a **stream of influence** that is faster, louder, and more persistent than anything we can match without a plan.

This chapter is designed to **coach parents and educators separately** while building a shared understanding of the risks of **untrained tech use**, and the supernatural solutions offered through the curriculum's 11 chapters.

⚠ 1. Shortened Attention Span

What's Happening:

Digital content is often designed for rapid, bite-sized engagement. Children swipe, scroll, and shift constantly. Their brains are trained to move quickly but not to stay still.

Why It Matters:

When attention spans are underdeveloped, children struggle with:

- Homework or reading time
- Following instructions
- Processing spiritual or emotional conversations
- Finishing goals

👥 For Parents:

At home, you may notice your child is "bored" easily or can't play without jumping between apps or toys.

Coaching Strategy:

Start introducing *Chapter 2 – Biblical and Scientific Meditation* through phone-guided meditations and breathwork audio. Make it a 5-minute routine after school or before bedtime.

Curriculum Link:

Meditation helps reset the nervous system. Over time, it retrains the brain to be still, present, and focused—especially powerful when tied to Philippians 4:8.

◉lı For Educators:

In class, students may fidget, ask "What's next?" constantly, or give up mid-task.

Coaching Strategy:

Use **Chapter 3 – Executive Functioning Skills** to introduce timer-based focus challenges. Let students set their phone timers to complete one task at a time. Celebrate completions, not just performance.

Curriculum Link:

Teaching focus through executive functioning tools supports long-term academic confidence and builds mental endurance.

⚠ 2. Comparison & Anxiety

What's Happening:

Social media and visual platforms introduce children to curated lives that seem perfect, filtered, or unattainable. This builds insecurity, jealousy, and shame—often silently.

Why It Matters:

Children lose confidence, avoid risks, and develop false beliefs about their worth.

👤👤 For Parents:

You may hear your child say things like, "I'm not good enough," "They have more," or "I'll never look like that."

Coaching Strategy:

Activate *Chapter 1 – Who Am I and What Powers Do I Possess?* by encouraging your child to create a "Unique Me" digital collage. Use their phone to take pictures of their strengths, friends, favorite books, and affirmations.

Curriculum Link:

This chapter teaches that identity is found within—God-given, not app-driven. Visual reinforcement increases resilience.

⬤❚❙ For Educators:

Students may compare project results, avoid speaking up, or disengage during collaborative work.

Coaching Strategy:

Introduce *Chapter 10 – Social Skills* and guide students through "Voice of Value" reflections—short video or audio journal entries about something they did well that day.

Curriculum Link:

Teaching students to affirm their own growth cultivates emotional intelligence and healthy comparison habits.

•

⚠ 3. Emotional Dysregulation

What's Happening:

Constant screen time floods the brain with stimulation but provides no space to process emotions. When the phone is taken away, children may erupt or spiral emotionally.

Why It Matters:

Emotional outbursts are not simply behavioral—they are the result of unprocessed feelings and over-activated nervous systems.

👥 For Parents:

Meltdowns over small things? Sudden shutdowns? These are signs your child's emotional systems are overloaded.

Coaching Strategy:

Use *Chapter 11 – Good Habits* to create daily routines anchored in stability, including time for meditation, quiet journaling, or creative phone use (photo journaling, music reflection).

Curriculum Link:

Good habits create the emotional rhythm children need. Phone use becomes a calming bridge, not a chaos trigger.

👍 For Educators:

Classroom transitions become emotional flashpoints. Students may withdraw, lash out, or resist correction.

Coaching Strategy:

Use *Chapter 9 – Physical Education* to introduce movement resets (stretch + deep breathing), and integrate music/movement breaks accessed through classroom-approved audio apps.

Curriculum Link:

Linking physical movement and emotional reset is essential for classroom self-regulation.

⚠ 4. Digital Avoidance & Escapism

What's Happening:

When phones become the "easy way out" of boredom, responsibility, or discomfort, students use them to escape—leading to compulsive behavior and decreased resilience.

Why It Matters:

If unaddressed, this becomes addiction. Phones become a "need" rather than a tool, leading to loss of motivation and dependence.

👥 For Parents:

You may notice your child disappearing into their screen after school and refusing to participate in real-world chores or conversations.

Coaching Strategy:

Incorporate *Chapter 4 – GOP FROG Time* by having your child use a phone goal-setting app to choose one task each morning and reflect on it each evening. They'll use the device to move **toward responsibility**, not away from it.

Curriculum Link:

Setting goals transforms a phone from a toy into a mission planner.

🍎 For Educators:

You may see students mentally disengaged unless screens are involved. They struggle with persistence and initiative.

Coaching Strategy:

Leverage *Chapter 5 – The Importance of Reading* by integrating digital reading reflection tools. Let them record themselves reading aloud, then discussing key themes. Phones become a mirror of effort.

Curriculum Link:

Reading + tech = power when it's used to elevate comprehension, not escape it.

⚠ 5. Identity Loss in the Algorithm

What's Happening:

Children shaped only by digital content begin to mimic online behavior. Without real-life anchors, they lose awareness of who they are outside the screen.

👤👤 For Parents:

Has your child started mimicking slang, style, or beliefs from the internet? Are they losing connection with their unique self?

Coaching Strategy:

Apply *Chapter 6 – The Importance of History* by helping them create a "My Legacy Timeline" on their device, using family stories, Bible verses, and personal moments of growth.

Curriculum Link:

When students understand the past, they find their place in the present—and reclaim their future identity.

🍎 For Educators:

Students may struggle to express original ideas or default to "internet speak."

Coaching Strategy:

Engage *Chapter 8 – The Importance of Science* and task students with creating digital investigations: "How does screen time affect the brain?" This empowers them to critique the very tools shaping them.

Curriculum Link:

Scientific inquiry invites self-awareness and replaces imitation with exploration.

🔍 In Summary

Untrained tech use is a crisis of formation.

But with intentional, curriculum-based coaching, we don't have to fear the phone.

- We can redeem it.
- We can retrain the brain.
- We can rebuild attention.
- We can restore joy.
- We can reaffirm purpose.

The following chapters show how.

📖 Chapter 2:
Digital Addiction

Warning Signs, Prevention, and Correction for Parents and Educators

"What we call 'screen time'—our kids call life. So let's help them live it with clarity, courage, and control."

What Is Digital Addiction?

Digital addiction refers to compulsive, excessive, or emotionally dependent engagement with phones and screens that interferes with everyday functioning, relationships, or growth. It is not a diagnosis in this guide—but it is a very real **developmental threat** to our children's ability to focus, relate, and live with purpose.

⚠ Disclaimer

This guide is not written by a licensed medical provider, therapist, or psychologist. It is designed as a **coaching tool** to support families and educators with faith-rooted, curriculum-aligned guidance. If your child or student shows signs of emotional distress, obsessive behavior, or withdrawal, please seek professional support from a licensed counselor or pediatric specialist.

🚨 Warning Signs of Digital Addiction

Each sign below is followed by a breakdown for **parents** and **educators**, and a curriculum-based coaching response.

---

1. Preoupation with Devices

Child is constantly thinking about their phone—even when not using it.

👥 For Parents:

Watch for signs like reaching for their phone first thing in the morning, repeatedly asking for screen time, or complaining of boredom without it.

✅ *Use Chapter 4: GOP FROG TIME*

Have your child make a "phone use schedule" as part of their daily goal planning. This puts boundaries **in their hands**, guided by your values.

For Educators:

Students may constantly ask, "When's the next break?" or glance at pockets/desks for their phone. They may lose focus unless tech is involved.

✅ *Use Chapter 3: Executive Functioning Skills*

Teach phone use as a **task-based tool**, not a default accessory. Example: "Use your device to track your progress—not to avoid your project."

---

2. Loss of Interest in Offline Activities

Child no longer enjoys hobbies, books, outdoor play, or conversation unless a screen is involved.

For Parents:

You may notice your child avoids family game nights, rushes through meals, or resists outdoor time. They may say, "That's boring" to anything non-digital.

✅ *Use Chapter 5: The Importance of Reading*

Let them listen to audiobooks on their phone. Then have them **create a voice note reflection** summarizing what they learned.

Also introduce **Chapter 9: Physical Education**

Challenge them to record fun outdoor fitness videos for the family, turning movement into mission.

◢▮▮ For Educators:

Watch for students who decline group activities, remain disengaged in hands-on projects, or express disinterest unless technology is involved.

✅ *Use Chapter 8: The Importance of Science*

Have students conduct a personal experiment: "What happens to my energy and mood on screen-free days vs. screen-heavy days?" Let their phones help track and report real findings.

---

3. Emotional Disruption When Denied Access

Child becomes angry, anxious, sad, or panicked when their device is removed or limited.

👤👤 For Parents:

Watch for mood swings, yelling, or emotional collapse when you say, "Time to turn it off." Their nervous system may have become **dependent on stimulation**.

✅ *Use Chapter 2: Meditation*

Create a calming bedtime and tech wind-down routine using gentle meditations and affirmations played from the device itself. Reframe "phone time" as "peace time."

●‖ For Educators:

If a student cannot refocus or self-regulate after being told to put a device away, the classroom may become emotionally unstable.

✅ *Use Chapter 11: Good Habits*

Model and build emotional stamina: "We put the phone away now. Let's breathe, reflect, and return to the present." Reinforce with a visible digital or paper-based habit tracker.

---

4. Deception About Screen Use

Child hides screen time, deletes history, or lies about how long they've been using the phone.

👤👤 For Parents:

You may find hidden apps, sneaky behavior at night, or "I was just checking something" when confronted.

✅ *Use Chapter 1: Who Am I and What Powers Do I Possess?*

Build trust-based identity: "You are powerful enough to be honest." Invite them to help design their own tech boundary agreement and commit to it **with you**.

📱 For Educators:

Watch for students hiding devices under desks, switching apps quickly, or "pretending" to do schoolwork.

✅ *Use Chapter 6: The Importance of History*

Invite students to reflect: "What kind of digital footprint do I want to leave?" Connect past decisions to future consequences.

🛡️ Preventing Digital Addiction: Core Strategies

Here are proactive steps both parents and educators can take to **build a tech relationship that fosters growth—not addiction**.

👤👤 For Parents:

1. **Create a Phone Purpose Statement**

2. "We use our phones to grow, learn, and reflect—not to avoid, hide, or escape." Post this on the fridge.

3. **Tech-Free Anchor Zones**

4. Meals, bedrooms, and family devotionals should be sacred spaces. Use **Chapter 11: Good Habits** to practice daily digital rhythm.

5. **Scheduled Reflection Time**

6. Each night, use voice memos or journals to reflect: "How did I use my phone to grow today?" Encourage honesty without judgment.

7. **Involve Them in Boundaries**

8. Let your child co-create limits using planning tools from **Chapter 4**. It gives them ownership.

📶 For Educators:

1. **Tech on Purpose Only**

2. Tie all phone use to chapter objectives: "Today we use our phones for our reading reflections and to document our FROG Time goals."

3. **Build Restorative Habits**

4. Use moments of regulation (like **Chapter 2: Meditation**) to reconnect students when they're emotionally overwhelmed by devices.

5. **Student-Led Showcase Projects**

6. Let students create weekly content (videos, digital collages, goal trackers) that demonstrate what they're learning about themselves—not just what they consume.

7. **Coach, Don't Control**

8. Correct phone misuse with reflection, not shame: "What were you hoping to feel when you picked up your phone just now?"

Correcting Digital Dependency Gently (When It's Already a Problem)

If your child or student already shows signs of dependence:

Step 1: Don't panic. Don't punish.

Start by replacing—not removing.

Add meditation, journaling, and reflection practices **before** cutting back time.

Step 2: Offer Connection, Not Control

Ask: "What's really going on when you want to be on your phone all day?"

Offer compassion and redirect them toward identity-building projects from **Ch. 1, 5, or 10**.

Step 3: Invite Real-Life Leadership

Have them lead a digital wellness challenge at home or school. Let them **teach others** how they're overcoming addiction. This turns struggle into strength.

📖 Chapter 3:
How the 11 Chapters Guide Purposeful Phone Use

"These aren't just lessons—these are lifelong strategies. And the phone can support every one."

This chapter is written to **equip and coach parents and educators** to intentionally connect every chapter of the *Unlocking Your Great Potential Within You* curriculum to modern digital life. By doing so, phones become:

- Tools for transformation
- Instruments of reflection
- Anchors for identity
- Planners for peace

Each section below includes:

- ✓ The chapter's purpose
- 📱 A purposeful phone strategy
- 👤👤 Parent coaching points
- 🍎 Educator coaching points

📖 Chapter 1: Who Am I and What Powers Do I Possess?

✓ **Purpose:** Build identity, self-worth, and uniqueness rooted in God's truth—not culture.

📱 **Phone Strategy:**

Use the camera and voice recorder to create a **"Power Within Me" project** where children record or photograph the traits, habits, and gifts that make them powerful.

👤👥 **Parents:**

Have your child create a "My Strengths" photo album and add one picture a week showing them doing something great—being kind, solving a problem, showing joy.

🎓🍎 **Educators:**

Have students record 30-second "Power Statements" using their devices:

"I am strong because I…"

Create a gallery or class playlist for celebration.

📕 Chapter 2: Biblical and Scientific Meditation

✅ **Purpose:** Teach children how to calm their minds, connect with God, and reset their thoughts.

📱 **Phone Strategy:**

Use audio Bible meditations, scripture playlists, or calming music apps during transitions, bedtime, or rest time.

👤👥 **Parents:**

Make meditation part of your child's nighttime routine. Let them choose a 3–5 minute calming track and teach them to say:

"Peace lives in me."

🍎📶 **Educators:**

Begin class with a daily **digital pause**—use student devices (with headphones) to access an approved 2-minute breathing or scripture reflection.

📓 Chapter 3: Executive Functioning Skills

✅ **Purpose:** Build self-control, memory, organization, planning, and flexible thinking.

📱 **Phone Strategy:**

Teach children to use reminders, task lists, calendar tools, or photo reminders for organizing schoolwork and routines.

👤👥 **Parents:**

Let your child take a photo of their cleaned room, completed reading, or organized school bag. Celebrate task completion digitally!

🍎 **Educators:**

Have students use their phones to snap pictures of whiteboard instructions, upcoming assignments, or steps in a process.

📓 Chapter 4: GOP FROG TIME – Goal-Oriented Planning

✅ **Purpose:** Teach students to prioritize, plan, and stick with short- and long-term goals.

📱 **Phone Strategy:**

Use planning apps or the built-in notes/reminders app to list daily goals with checkmarks or emojis.

👤👥 **Parents:**

Every morning, let your child use your phone (or theirs) to record a voice note:

"Today I will focus on…"

Listen to it again before bed to reflect.

🍎📊 **Educators:**

Start the week with students recording one weekly goal related to the curriculum. Let them revisit it Friday to evaluate progress.

📖 Chapter 5: The Importance of Reading

✅ **Purpose:** Strengthen literacy, comprehension, and the love of learning.

📱 **Phone Strategy:**

Use audiobook apps, read-aloud recordings, and digital storytime to bring stories to life. Record themselves reading too!

👤👥 **Parents:**

Have your child read a paragraph aloud and record themselves. Encourage them to listen back and reflect:

"How did I sound confident?"

🍎📊 **Educators:**

Assign a "Read & Reflect" task where students record 30 seconds summarizing what they read—connecting reading to speaking skills.

Chapter 6: The Importance of History

✓ **Purpose:** Teach children how past experiences shape current identity and vision for the future.

📱 **Phone Strategy:**

Use phones to take photos of local landmarks, record family stories, or create a personal timeline using apps or slideshows.

👤👤 **Parents:**

Have your child interview a grandparent or elder on your phone. Ask questions like, "What habits helped you become strong?"

🍎📊 **Educators:**

Plan digital history scavenger hunts. Let students use their phones to research local facts and present them with visuals.

📖 Chapter 7: The Importance of Math

✅ **Purpose:** Train the mind for logical thinking, problem-solving, and persistence.

📱 **Phone Strategy:**

Use camera functions to photograph and annotate math steps. Use calculator apps for self-checking (with explanation).

👤👤 **Parents:**

Have your child calculate daily life math: recipes, store budgets, or sleep hours. Record the process.

🍎📊 **Educators:**

Encourage students to explain their math thinking via short "math talk" videos to deepen conceptual understanding.

📖 Chapter 8: The Importance of Science

✅ **Purpose:** Inspire curiosity, experimentation, and critical thinking.

📱 **Phone Strategy:**

Use the phone as a **science notebook**—to record nature, document experiments, or track health/sleep habits.

👥 **Parents:**

Let your child video-record a "wonder moment" outdoors. Have them explain what they see or want to explore.

🍎 **Educators:**

Assign digital field observation logs during experiments or field days. Use photos to track changes, patterns, or outcomes.

📖 Chapter 9: The Importance of Physical Education

✅ **Purpose:** Connect body movement with mental clarity and emotional regulation.

📱 **Phone Strategy:**

Use movement-based apps or workout trackers. Let students create their own workout videos to demonstrate knowledge.

👤👥 **Parents:**

Create a "Fitness Friday" challenge: have your child create or follow a 3-minute activity video and share their effort.

🍎📊 **Educators:**

Assign group physical education videos. Students can choreograph, demonstrate, and lead their own fitness routines.

📓 Chapter 10: The Importance of Social Skills

✓ **Purpose:** Develop empathy, communication, kindness, and conflict resolution.

📱 **Phone Strategy:**

Use phones for gratitude logs, encouragement notes, or audio "kindness missions" (recording compliments or encouragement).

👥 **Parents:**

Have your child record a kind message for a friend or teacher. Encourage "digital encouragement" as a weekly habit.

🍎 **Educators:**

Use peer-to-peer voice memos for feedback and affirmation:

"I noticed that you helped…" or "You worked hard today because…"

📓 Chapter 11: Good Habits

✅ **Purpose:** Instill consistency, personal discipline, and daily routines that align with purpose and peace.

📱 **Phone Strategy:**

Use digital habit trackers, journal apps, and prayer alerts. Let students "track the habits that build their future."

👤👥 **Parents:**

Pick 3 daily habits and track them using emoji checklists or habit apps: prayer, meditation, kindness, clean-up.

🍎 **Educators:**

Create a class-wide "Good Habits Dashboard" (paper or digital) and let students log personal progress using their devices.

🔄 Final Word: Curriculum as a Compass

These 11 chapters are not standalone lessons—they're **spiritual formation pathways**. Each one invites the student to become more reflective, more grounded, and more equipped to lead their thoughts, actions, and choices—even on a device.

When integrated into phone habits, the curriculum:

- Builds internal voice
- Shapes decision-making
- Reinforces boundaries
- Activates confidence
- Fosters responsibility
- Models the **mind of Christ** in a digital world

📖 Chapter 4:
Purposeful Phone Use for Ages 3–5:
Prevention and Modeling

"Little eyes are watching. Little hands are learning. And what we model becomes what they mirror."

✅ Chapter Purpose:

Children between ages 3 and 5 are highly impressionable. They do not yet have a personal sense of time, self-regulation, or long-term decision-making. However, they are watching closely—and absorbing how the adults around them use phones.

This age group is **not ready to manage a device independently**, but they **are ready to learn what phones are for** when modeled intentionally.

That's why this chapter focuses on:

- **Preventing digital overexposure**
- **Replacing screen-time habits with connection-based habits**
- **Modeling peace, purpose, and praise when using devices**

👥 Parent Coaching: Teaching by Modeling

🎯 Guiding Principle:

Your phone habits are shaping theirs—even when you think they're not paying attention.

🔄 Replace "Silence by Screen" with "Silence by Peace"

Too often, phones are handed to toddlers or preschoolers to calm them down. But **the phone should never be their first regulator—you should be.**

Prevention Tip:

Instead of saying, "Here, play with this," say:

"Let's sit down and listen to something calming together."

✅ Use *Chapter 2: Meditation*

Play a short breathing exercise or scripture lullaby on your phone. Then put the phone down and breathe together.

📷 Build a "Good Habits Album"

Use *Chapter 11: Good Habits* by taking pictures of your child:

- Brushing their teeth
- Putting away toys
- Hugging a sibling
- Sitting peacefully during story time

Show them their "Super Habit Album" at the end of each week.

📱 Make Your Own Phone Use Visible and Intentional

Narrate what you're doing:

"I'm using my phone to listen to a Bible verse."

"Let's take a picture of the flowers God made today!"

When children see phones used for worship, creativity, and peace—they don't associate it only with games and cartoons.

⬤ Avoid These Common Pitfalls:

- **Don't use the phone to end tantrums.** Teach self-soothing instead (deep breathing, hugs, quiet music).

- **Don't treat the phone as a reward.** Treat connection and calm as the reward.

- **Don't leave screens unsupervised.** Even "kid-friendly" apps can deliver unsafe or overstimulating content.

Educator Coaching: Creating a Safe, Screen-Supported Classroom

Guiding Principle:

Phones in the classroom at this age should be **used by teachers—not by students.**

This is your opportunity to shape their earliest relationship with tech as **collaborative, calming, and constructive**.

📱 Approved Educator Use of Devices:

1. Audio Affirmations or Bible Verses

Play a 1–2 minute clip to start or end the day. Connect it to *Chapter 1: Who Am I?*

"God made me special. I have good thoughts."

---

2. Photo Journals of Progress

Use your phone to take pictures of the children engaging in:

- Cleaning up

- Sharing with friends

- Completing a story or activity

- This supports *Chapter 10: Social Skills* and *Chapter 5: Reading*.

Create a class slideshow or "Kindness Wall."

3. Guided Movement & Meditation Breaks

Use music apps or kid-friendly YouTube tracks to lead:

- Yoga stretches

- Jump-and-count songs

- Dance-and-pause games

This connects to *Chapter 9: Physical Education* in a developmentally appropriate way.

⬤ Avoid These in the Classroom:

- Never allow free phone or tablet use at this age.

- Do not use phones as behavior management tools ("You can watch if you sit still.")

- Do not model screen distraction—keep your own tech use purposeful and visible.

Integrated Daily Routine for Ages 3–5

Here's how the curriculum and device modeling can work together in a typical day:

Time	Activity	Phone Use (Adult Only)
Morning Greeting	"Power Within Me" Affirmation	Play audio while students breathe or repeat
Reading Circle	"Read & Reflect" story time	Snap pictures of attentive listening for later display
Movement Break	Gross motor skill play	Lead movement using music/audio
Quiet Time	Meditation story or worship music	Soft scripture audio via phone, no screen
Afternoon Reflection	Praise for good habits	Show photo progress or play recorded thank-yous

✦ Final Word for This Age Group

Children ages 3–5 are not digital citizens yet.

They are **digital observers**.

And what they observe… they will become.

Use every moment to model a device that reflects **peace**, **presence**, **joy**, and **purpose**. That's how we prevent tech addiction **before it starts**—and lay a strong foundation for everything else to come.

📖 Chapter 5:
Purposeful Phone Use for Ages 6–9:
Training and Structure

"This is the season to build rhythms—because rhythms turn into habits, and habits form character."

✅ Chapter Purpose:

Children between ages 6 and 9 are in a **critical learning window** where the brain is absorbing **structure**, **rules**, **rewards**, and **the beginnings of independence**. While they may not yet fully understand long-term consequences, they can understand **how to follow a rhythm**, **check a list**, and **feel proud of progress**.

This is the age where **purposeful phone use** is introduced with **training, boundaries, and joy**—not fear or shame.

👥 Parent Coaching: Digital Parenting with Structure & Praise

🎯 Guiding Principle:

This is not the age of "free phone time." It's the age of **"guided phone time with purpose."**

Phones become tools for:

- Organizing daily habits
- Celebrating good decisions
- Building reflection and planning
- Practicing meditation and memory

Practice Habit-Building with Chapter 11 – Good Habits

Choose 2–3 simple daily habits: "Read," "Pray," "Clean up."

Track them in a **habit app**, sticker chart, or phone note checklist. Review each night.

✅ Celebrate: "You did your habits 5 days in a row! That's the power of consistency!"

➤📱 Use Their Voice to Reflect – Chapter 1 & 4

Have your child record short voice notes:

- "What went well today?"
- "What's one goal I have for tomorrow?"
- "How did I show kindness?"

This aligns with *Chapter 4 – GOP FROG TIME* and *Chapter 1 – Identity*, helping them reflect with language.

📚 Use Storytime Apps to Expand Imagination – Chapter 5

Let your child listen to Bible-based or values-driven audiobooks. Then have them draw or record what they learned.

✓ This develops comprehension and listening—a foundational executive function.

💡 Reinforce with Tech-Free Rewards:

Phones should not be the reward—**growth is**.

"You used your phone to grow. Now let's go play outside!"

🍎 Educator Coaching: Routines that Reinforce Reflection

🎯 Guiding Principle:

This is the age of **training, not just reminding**. Children thrive when tech time is embedded into **meaningful structure**.

Start with "Purpose Prompts"

As students enter the classroom, have them reflect:

"What's one way I'll use my phone to grow today?"

Write it on a board or input into a classroom journal app.

Use Chapter 3 – Executive Functioning

Assign structured phone-based tasks like:

- Taking a picture of their work
- Setting a timer for focus
- Recording a list of materials for tomorrow's project

Let tech support their **mental planning** skills.

♀ Lead with Meditation – Chapter 2

During transitions, play a 2-minute "brain break" from your phone. You can use:

- Worship instrumentals

- Deep breathing tracks

- Guided Philippians 4:8 mantras

Students will learn: **phones can calm me—not just hype me.**

🎙 Celebrate Reflection with Audio Journaling

Once a week, let students record a 15–30 second check-in:

"One thing I've learned is…"

"I used good habits when I…"

Share a few highlights during circle time (with consent) to build pride and emotional voice.

▦ Weekly Routine Example (6–9-Year-Olds)

Day	Phone Use Objective	Curriculum Connection
Monday	Record a weekly goal	Ch. 4 – Goal Setting
Tuesday	Track 3 habits in habit app	Ch. 11 – Good Habits
Wednesday	Read & Reflect (voice note or photo)	Ch. 5 – Reading
Thursday	Meditation with reflection	Ch. 2 – Meditation
Friday	Photo journal of something they're proud of	Ch. 1 – Identity

✔ Final Word for Parents & Educators (Ages 6–9)

This is the age of *training with joy.*

It's not about restriction—it's about **repetition**.

Let the phone become a reflection of your child's **growth**, **values**, and **progress**—never just a reward for silence or a toy for boredom.

And remember, the phone is not just a mirror of distraction—it can become a **mirror of God's purpose** when used wisely.

📖 Chapter 6:
Purposeful Phone Use for Ages 10–13:
Reconstruction and Identity

"At this age, they're not just learning what to do—they're deciding who they are. Let's help them do both with intention."

✅ Chapter Purpose:

This age group often represents a digital **tipping point**. They are curious, capable, and emotionally open—but also highly vulnerable to comparison, insecurity, distraction, and overuse of devices for escapism.

If unhealthy habits began early, this is the age to **reconstruct a healthier relationship with tech**.

Phones become tools to:

- Reflect identity
- Organize thinking
- Deepen social understanding
- Manage emotional and spiritual growth
- Encourage safe expression and real ownership

👤👥 Parent Coaching: Reconstructing Identity with Purpose

🎯 Guiding Principle:

Your preteen no longer just mimics—they're beginning to internalize. Your job now is to **coach with care, not just control**.

🎥 Build Power With Reflection Videos – Chapter 1

Have your child create weekly video entries:

"This week I showed my power by…"

"One thing I did well today was…"

"A mistake I made and how I handled it…"

These entries become a **digital mirror of growth**—a way to shape identity through voice and choice.

♀ Create Daily Reset Routines – Chapter 2

Let your child use their phone for **calm time**, not just screen time. Use:

- Scripture-based meditation
- Lo-fi worship playlists
- Breathing apps

You're helping them **reset from stimulation**, not escape into it.

▯ Encourage Planning and Accountability – Chapter 3 & 4

Help them use phone calendars or notes for:

- Homework reminders
- Spiritual routines (e.g., "Morning prayer time")
- Reading goals
- Daily to-do lists

This models independence **without isolation**.

💬 Engage in Tech Talks Weekly

Each week, ask:

"How did your phone help or distract you this week?"

"What did you see that made you feel good? What didn't?"

"How are you showing up online?"

You're not checking in to control—you're checking in to **connect**.

🍎 Educator Coaching: Building Executive Identity

🎯 Guiding Principle:

These students want freedom—but they need structure and purpose behind it. You're teaching them to lead themselves digitally.

📱 Use Curriculum-Aligned Tools:

- **Chapter 5 – Reading:**

- → Let them record audio summaries of books or stories

- **Chapter 6 – History:**

- → Assign heritage-based digital presentations: "What in my past helps shape my future?"

- **Chapter 8 – Science:**

- → Use phones for digital experiments, photo data, or environmental tracking

---

🎙 Reflection + Ownership = Empowerment

Teach students to record and own their progress using:

- Weekly audio reflections
- Digital goal trackers
- Self-assessed behavior charts (with emoji sliders or stars)

Give students a voice to shape their day—not just receive it.

● Guide Social Safety – Chapter 10

Teach students how to:

- Respond to text/social messages with integrity
- Use positive digital language
- Block/report in unsafe situations
- Ask questions like: "Would I say this in person?"

Use classroom role-play scenarios and digital citizenship check-ins.

Weekly Themes for Ages 10–13 (Curriculum-Connected)

Day	Focus	Phone Use	Chapter Tie-In
Monday	Identity Check	Record power video	Chapter 1
Tuesday	Emotional Reset	Midday meditation	Chapter 2
Wednesday	Academic Ownership	Set weekly goals	Chapter 3 & 4
Thursday	Voice & Growth	Audio summary or vlog	Chapter 5 & 6
Friday	Good Habit Wrap-Up	Log tracker & reflect	Chapter 11

✅ Final Word for Parents & Educators (Ages 10–13)

This age group is **ready for responsibility**, but it must be wrapped in routine, reflection, and **relational connection**.

Don't aim to control the device.

Teach them to **control themselves**—and let the phone become proof of it.

They don't just need boundaries.

They need **blueprints.**

They don't just need reminders.

They need **reasons.**

And they don't just need discipline.

They need to believe they have **power within**—to lead their own digital lives.

📖 Chapter 7:
Purposeful Phone Use for Teens (Ages 14+): Empowerment and Digital Leadership

"At this stage, the question isn't whether they'll use their phones—it's how they'll use them to lead."

✅ Chapter Purpose:

Teenagers are digital natives. Most already use phones daily for social, school, or creative purposes. But left without structure, phones can become tools for:

- Escape
- Performance
- Addiction
- Isolation
- Validation

This chapter equips **parents** and **educators** to help teens **reconstruct**, **refocus**, and **reclaim** their phones as tools of growth, identity, and leadership.

This is not the time for fear-based rules. It is the time for:

- Partnership
- Purpose
- Planning
- Practice
- Praise

👥 Parent Coaching: From Regulation to Leadership

🎯 Guiding Principle:

Your teen is not a child anymore. You're no longer just regulating—you're **releasing**. But release must come with wisdom.

Phones must become:

- A planning system
- A reflection tool
- A content creation platform for good
- A mirror of their values—not someone else's

▤ 1. Personal Digital Planning – Chapter 3 & 4

Teens should use phones as their **command center**:

- Time-block study hours
- Track reading with notes or checklists
- Set spiritual goals (daily scripture, prayer timers)
- Plan fitness or social commitments

You're helping them **practice future discipline today**.

---

2. Reflection is Power – Chapter 1

Ask your teen to create a private vlog, podcast, or audio journal on their phone:

"What did I learn this week?"

"What mindset am I working on?"

"How did I use my phone to live better?"

Encourage expression that isn't filtered for likes—but rooted in truth.

🚫 3. Weekly Phone Review (Together)

Use screen time tracking to evaluate:

- Time spent
- Top 3 apps
- Most valuable use
- Least valuable use

"Let's look at this together and make a plan."

"What do you want to change?"

This invites **responsibility** without shame.

🎯 4. Lead at Home

Invite them to:

- Design a tech-free family dinner
- Lead the family in a meditation or scripture
- Create a digital slideshow of gratitude moments

You're moving them from user → **leader**.

📲 Educator Coaching: Building Digital Influence with Intention

🎯 Guiding Principle:

Teens don't want lectures—they want leadership. Show them how their phones can represent **who they are and who they're becoming**.

Phones become:

- Creativity tools
- Social impact platforms
- Data trackers
- Personal libraries
- Character portfolios

🎥 1. Showcase Identity Through Content – Chapter 1

Let students create:

- Visual collages about their strengths
- "I Am" spoken word videos
- Digital art portfolios
- Testimonies of how they overcame personal challenges

Use safe classroom safe-sharing platforms (Google Sites, Flip, etc.) to display purpose-driven digital expression.

📕 2. Use Phones for Academic Integration

- Math: Graph real-world data from screen time or sleep
- Science: Log hydration, step count, or food intake
- Reading: Record book reflections or create digital quote boards
- History: Compare their own journey to leaders or timelines

Their phone becomes their personal textbook and lab notebook.

🖊 3. Peer Mentorship

Allow students to create weekly:

- Encouragement videos
- Peer tutorials ("How to plan my week," "How to deal with stress")
- Group reflections on meditation habits

Assign them roles like:

- Digital Wellness Coach
- Tech Organizer
- Reflection Leader

♡ 4. Real-Time Digital Citizenship – Chapter 10

Let students explore:

- Who sees what I post?

- Does this reflect my faith?

- Am I building someone up or tearing someone down?

Use real examples, group think-alouds, and open conversation to shape mindset.

⬚ Weekly Leadership Routine for Teens

Day	Theme	Phone Activity	Curriculum Link
Monday	Planning	Time-block schedule	Chapter 4
Tuesday	Wellness	Meditation & sleep log	Chapter 2 & 9
Wednesday	Voice	Record personal reflection	Chapter 1
Thursday	Impact	Encourage others digitally	Chapter 10
Friday	Review	Screen time analysis	Chapter 11

✔️ Final Word for Parents & Educators (Ages 14+)

Your teen is growing. And now, so is their **influence**.

It's time to help them:

- **Lead online** the same way they want to lead in life
- **Protect their mental space** as powerfully as they guard their schedule
- **Use their phone** to build, bless, and become—not just scroll, compare, and survive

Phones can be a **mirror** of brokenness—or a **launchpad** of purpose.

Let's help them choose wisely.

📖 Chapter 8:
Implementing the Curriculum:
Purposeful Phone Use Across All 11 Chapters

"The curriculum was never meant to live on paper. It was made to breathe through practice—in hearts, habits, and homes."

✅ **Chapter Purpose:**

This chapter walks parents, educators, and learning facilitators through **exact ways to apply phone use purposefully** for each curriculum chapter. You'll be guided on how to build routines, reinforce reflection, and create alignment between phone use and the **supernatural skills** taught in:

1. Meditation

2. Executive Functioning

3. Good Habits

For each chapter, you'll find:

- 🔍 **Goal/Purpose**
- 🏠 **Home Application**
- 🍎 **Classroom Application**
- 🌍 **Community Extension**

📘 Chapter 1: Who Am I and What Powers Do I Possess?

🔍 **Goal:** Establish identity, voice, and inner strength.

🏠 **Home:**

- Record a 1-minute "Power Statement" video each week (e.g., "I am powerful when I...").
- Use the photo album to create a "Power Collage" of accomplishments, kind actions, or scriptures.

🍎 **Classroom:**

- Students record audio introductions: "Three things that make me unique."
- Display photo collages on classroom boards or slideshows.

🌍 **Community:**

- Interview a family or church leader on what made them strong growing up. Record and reflect.

📖 Chapter 2: Biblical and Scientific Meditation

🔍 **Goal:** Teach calming techniques, emotional regulation, and spiritual reflection.

🏠 **Home:**

- Use a 5-minute scripture meditation app before bed.
- Record a personal mantra (e.g., "I am calm. I am connected. I am focused.")

🍎📶 **Classroom:**

- Start or close each day with a 3-minute group meditation from a phone or speaker.
- Use scripture journaling apps for quiet writing time.

🌍 **Community:**

- Lead a "Community Calm" circle at a church, camp, or family event using your phone to play scripture-based peace meditations.

📓 Chapter 3: Executive Functioning Skills

🔍 **Goal:** Strengthen planning, memory, focus, and task completion.

🏠 **Home:**

- Use phone reminders or alarms for tasks (cleaning, reading, prayer time).
- Take photos of completed checklists and review together.

🍎 **Classroom:**

- Students use phones to photograph instructions or deadlines.
- Teach them to use calendar apps to plan their assignments.

🌍 **Community:**

- Help organize a service event and assign digital roles (checklist manager, reminder sender, photo capturer).

📓 Chapter 4: GOP FROG TIME (Goal-Oriented Planning)

🔍 **Goal:** Prioritize daily goals and tasks with focus and accountability.

🏠 **Home:**

- Each morning, use the voice recorder to state the day's goals.
- Use stickers or emojis to celebrate each completed task.

🍎📊 **Classroom:**

- Start "GOP FROG" time with phone alarms set for a goal period (20–30 min).
- Reflect using digital forms or goal journals.

🌍 **Community:**

- Plan a short-term community project (garden day, clean-up) and document each phase with digital reflections and images.

📖 Chapter 5: The Importance of Reading

🔍 **Goal:** Cultivate comprehension, literacy joy, and personal connection to stories.

🏠 **Home:**

- Listen to audiobooks together and pause for reflection.
- Record story retellings in their own voice.

🍎 **Classroom:**

- Have students use phones to read aloud, then reflect: "What was the big idea?"
- Create digital "book reviews" using Flip or Google Forms.

🌍 **Community:**

- Visit a local library and create a visual "My Reading Adventure" diary with photos, book covers, and summaries.

📓 Chapter 6: The Importance of History

🔍 **Goal:** Build time awareness, legacy thinking, and social context.

🏠 **Home:**

- Research family history using voice memos or videos.
- Create a digital timeline using photos, birthdays, milestones, and maps.

🍎📊 **Classroom:**

- Use history apps or AR tours of historical landmarks.
- Record connections between personal and historical struggles.

🌍 **Community:**

- Visit a local museum, document the trip, and present lessons learned digitally.

📓 Chapter 7: The Importance of Math

🔍 **Goal:** Enhance problem-solving, logic, and number fluency.

🏠 Home:

- Use calculator apps to plan a grocery list or budget.
- Track screen time or bedtime with graphs made in Google Sheets.

🍎 Classroom:

- Teach students how to use calculator apps responsibly.
- Assign math story problems to solve and record with steps.

🌍 Community:

- Plan a bake sale or fundraiser with real-world budgeting and pricing activities.

📖 Chapter 8: The Importance of Science

🔍 **Goal:** Encourage observation, inquiry, and systems thinking.

🏠 **Home:**

- Track weather patterns or plant growth with phone photos and notes.
- Use voice memos for "I wonder why..." science questions.

🍎 **Classroom:**

- Let students document a science experiment step-by-step with phones.
- Create digital hypothesis journals.

🌍 **Community:**

- Record nature walks, environmental observations, and community clean-up efforts for presentations.

📕 Chapter 9: The Importance of Physical Education

🔍 **Goal:** Promote physical awareness, movement regulation, and mental reset through exercise.

🏠 Home:

- Let your child record a dance, stretching, or movement video.
- Use phone timers for circuit workouts or walking breaks.

🍎 Classroom:

- Use phones for digital PE logs. Record what movement helped with focus or emotions.
- Practice daily "active brain breaks."

🌍 Community:

- Host or attend a fitness event and record their participation. Share short clips or reflections.

📕 Chapter 10: The Importance of Social Skills

🔍 **Goal:** Build empathy, conversation skills, conflict resolution, and collaboration.

🏠 Home:

- Role-play text messaging and digital etiquette.
- Record "encouragement notes" as audio or video and send to relatives or friends.

🍎 Classroom:

- Facilitate peer feedback through classroom-friendly platforms.
- Use voice recordings for "How I helped a friend today" reflections.

🌍 Community:

- Interview a community helper (pastor, coach, neighbor) about how kindness or leadership changed their lives.

📕 Chapter 11: Good Habits

🔍 **Goal:** Create sustainable, self-regulated patterns for life success.

🏠 **Home:**

- Use habit tracking apps for prayer, reading, chores, water intake, or digital boundaries.
- Check in weekly as a family.

🍎 **Classroom:**

- Build a "Good Habit Leaderboard" where students earn points for consistency. Use simple digital badges or class charts.

🌍 **Community:**

- Showcase students' best habits in an end-of-program slideshow or portfolio.

✨ Final Word: Integration Over Isolation

Phones are not a threat when purpose guides their use. Each chapter of this curriculum has a digital application that:

- Reinforces the child's voice
- Documents the child's growth
- Connects technology with God's design for order, peace, purpose, and potential

We're not raising digital consumers.

We're raising creators.

We're not managing screen time.

We're managing **souls in the digital world.**

📖 Chapter 9:
Family Tech Planning:
At-Home Activity Toolkit

"The home is the first classroom. The dinner table is the first boardroom. And the phone can be the first leadership tool—if we train our children to use it with purpose."

✅ Chapter Purpose:

This chapter is a **hands-on guide** for families to implement the *Unlocking Your Great Potential Within You* curriculum in daily life—with phones serving as digital tools for:

- Goal setting
- Reflection
- Identity building
- Spiritual practice
- Healthy habit tracking

These at-home activities are organized by core curriculum areas and are designed for ages **3–5, 6–9, 10–13, and teens**. Each activity uses a phone with purpose, structure, and joy.

Family Tech Planning Principles

1. **Phones Are for Growth First, Entertainment Second**

2. "This tool helps us grow before it helps us relax."

3. **Technology Is Shared and Supervised**

4. Children do not privately manage phones—they collaborate with a parent on purpose.

5. **Each Use Must Connect to One of the 3 Supernatural Powers**

6. Meditation (Peace), Executive Functioning (Planning), Good Habits (Growth)

7. **Reflection Is Required**

8. Every task includes a conversation, recording, or visual to connect meaning and emotion.

♂ Meditation (Ch. 2)

Age Group	Activity	Phone Use
3–5	Quiet Time with God	Play a short calming track and sit together. End with hugs and deep breaths.
6–9	Midday Peace Reset	Set an alarm for a 3-minute breathing or Scripture pause. Record how they feel after.
10–13	Emotional Check-In	Use a mood tracker or reflection journal app. Discuss: "What helped you feel better today?"
Teens	Reflection Playlist	Curate worship songs or meditations for daily reset. Reflect through journaling or voice memos.

Executive Functioning (Ch. 3 & 4)

Age Group	Activity	Phone Use
3–5	Picture Planning	Take a photo of their morning routine. Review each step together.
6–9	Reminder Partner	Set reminders for key habits (prayer, reading, chores). Use stickers or emojis when completed.
10–13	Daily Planner	Use a notes app to plan the day. Include priority tasks, study time, and breaks.
Teens	Digital Time Blocking	Create a weekly calendar for school, sleep, habits, and personal development. Adjust as needed.

📖 Good Habits (Ch. 11)

Age Group	Activity	Phone Use
3–5	Good Habit Picture Book	Take photos of habits like brushing teeth or sharing toys. Create a visual routine chart.
6–9	3 Habit Tracker	Track reading, gratitude, and kindness with emojis or stars. Celebrate at week's end.
10–13	Weekly Review	Record what habits they practiced well. Reflect on challenges. Set one new habit goal.
Teens	Growth Reflection	Create weekly audio logs: "This week I grew by…" or "Next week I want to improve…"

💡 Family Phone Use Agreements

Create a shared "Family Tech Use Plan" with your child.

Sample Agreement (6–9):

"I will use my phone to help me read, pray, and complete my good habits. I will ask for help when I'm unsure. I will take breaks and talk to my family."

Sample Agreement (10–13):

"I understand that my phone is a tool, not a toy. I will use it to plan my day, reflect on my emotions, and grow my relationship with God and others. I will check in with my parent when needed."

Sample Agreement (Teens):

"I agree to manage my time wisely, use my phone to grow mentally and spiritually, and share openly with my family. I will lead myself—and honor God—in how I use this device."

👤👤👤👤 Building a Family Routine

Time of Day	Routine Name	Phone Use
Morning	Power Start	Voice record today's goals or affirmation: "I will be…"
Afternoon	Growth Check	Track one habit or reflection from the day
Evening	Peace Practice	Listen to a scripture, play calm music, or reflect with journaling
Sunday	Family Tech Talk	Review apps used, screen time reports, and talk about changes for next week

Final Word to Families

The goal is not to make your home screen-free.

The goal is to make your home **soul-safe**.

Let your children:

- Watch you grow with your phone
- Hear themselves reflect through their phone
- Track their greatness
- Plan with joy
- Practice peace

And when needed—rest, reset, and return to center.

This is **not digital parenting—it's spiritual parenting with digital tools**.

📖 Chapter 10:
Classroom Tech Planning: Purposeful Use in Schools and Summer Learning Programs

"We're not fighting tech in the classroom—we're forming character through it."

✅ Chapter Purpose:

This chapter empowers educators and summer program facilitators to implement the curriculum with **intention, structure, and purpose-driven digital tools**. It includes:

- Step-by-step classroom activity instructions
- Realistic student examples using updated character names
- Recommended apps and digital platforms
- Practical tech integration strategies

Daily Classroom Integration Model

Time	Routine	Purposeful Phone Use	Curriculum Connection
Morning	Power Start	Record daily goal or affirmation	Ch. 1, Ch. 4
Midday	Meditation Reset	Guided breathing or worship	Ch. 2
Work Blocks	Structured Academic Tasks	Timers, audio notes, documentation	Ch. 3, 5, 6, 7, 8
Afternoon	Reflection Journals	Audio journaling or digital logs	Ch. 10, 11
Friday	Digital Check-In	Weekly screen time + habit review	Ch. 3, 11

■ CHAPTER-BY-CHAPTER ACTIVITIES WITH EXAMPLES & TOOLS

■ Chapter 1 – Who Am I and What Powers Do I Possess?

🔍 **Objective:** Build student self-worth and personal identity.

Activity: Power Within Video Collage

■ Instructions:

- Students record 30-second clips: "I am powerful when I..."
- Compile with photos to create a class "Power Gallery."

📱 **Tools:** Flip, Canva, Adobe Express

💡 **Example:**

Kenlyn records, "I am a leader because I help my friends stay focused." Her video is added to a class highlight reel.

📕 Chapter 2 – Biblical and Scientific Meditation

🔍 **Objective:** Teach mindfulness and emotional regulation.

Activity: Midday Meditation Moment

📋 **Instructions:**

- Use a timer and play calming music or Philippians 4:8 affirmations.

- Lead 3-minute breathing or stretching break.

📱 **Tools:** Abide, Insight Timer, Spotify (Scripture playlists)

💡 **Example:**

Students return from recess, listen to a calming track, and write down how their body feels after.

■ Chapter 3 – Executive Functioning Skills

🔍 **Objective:** Strengthen task organization and mental flexibility.

Activity: Focus & Reflect Block

💼 **Instructions:**

- Students take photos of step-by-step tasks.

- Use a focus timer for 20–30 min of work.

- Record a 30-second check-in reflection.

📱 **Tools:** Forest, Todoist, Voice Memos

💡 **Example:**

Noah photographs each stage of his science journal, sets a 25-minute timer, and records: "I stayed focused the whole time!"

📓 Chapter 4 – *GOP FROG TIME*

🔍 **Objective:** Train students to prioritize and complete goals.

Activity: Daily Goal Tracker

📋 **Instructions:**

- Each morning, students log one goal using a checklist, notes app, or audio.

- End the day with a progress check and celebration.

📱 **Tools:** Apple Notes, Google Keep, Habitica

💡 **Example:**

Ahlani writes, "Be a kind friend today." At the end of the day, she says, "I helped three classmates and smiled more!"

📖 Chapter 5 – The Importance of Reading

🔍 **Objective:** Improve reading fluency and comprehension.

Activity: Audio Reading Log

📋 **Instructions:**

- Students record themselves reading a story aloud.

- Reflect on what happened or what they learned.

📱 **Tools:** Flip, Seesaw, Book Creator

💡 **Example:**

Students upload weekly recordings to Flip. They listen to one another and leave comments like, "Great voice expression!"

📖 Chapter 6 – The Importance of History

🔍 **Objective:** Help students connect personal history with community context.

Activity: "My Timeline" Digital Project

📋 **Instructions:**

- Students build a personal or family timeline using photos and audio stories.

- Share lessons or values passed down.

📱 **Tools:** Google Slides, iMovie, Adobe Express

💡 **Example:**

Nyrie includes family photos from a church anniversary and narrates, "My family taught me to serve with love."

📖 Chapter 7 – The Importance of Math

🔍 **Objective:** Encourage real-world application of data and numbers.

Activity: Screen Time Graph Challenge

📋 **Instructions:**

- Students track their weekly phone/app use.

- Graph and reflect: "What will I improve next week?"

📱 **Tools:** iPhone Screen Time, Google Sheets, Canva

💡 **Example:**

Mason sees he used YouTube for 10 hours. He creates a goal graph: "Next week, only 3 hours."

📖 Chapter 8 – The Importance of Science

🔍 **Objective:** Deepen observation, recording, and analytical skills.

Activity: Digital Science Journal

📋 **Instructions:**

- Students photograph or record experiment steps.

- Add captions and reflections after each stage.

📱 **Tools:** Google Docs, PicCollage, Science Journal app

💡 **Example:**

During a water-cycle activity, students photograph each experiment phase and explain the results.

📖 Chapter 9 – The Importance of Physical Education

🔍 **Objective:** Link movement to brain function and emotional health.

Activity: Daily Fitness Video Challenge

📋 **Instructions:**

- Students record or lead a short movement routine.

- Add captions or voiceovers explaining benefits.

📱 **Tools:** Pacer, iMovie, TikTok (with limits)

💡 **Example:**

Na'ima leads a "Stretch & Praise" warm-up and reflects, "I feel stronger when I move in joy."

📓 Chapter 10 – The Importance of Social Skills

🔍 **Objective:** Strengthen empathy, teamwork, and digital kindness.

Activity: Kindness Voice Notes

📋 **Instructions:**

- Record or send 30-second voice compliments to classmates.

- Reflect: "How did that make you feel?"

📱 **Tools:** Flip, Google Voice, ClassDojo

💡 **Example:**

Students record: "Thank you for helping me today, Ahlani!" The class reflects on how it feels to uplift others.

📖 Chapter 11 – *Good Habits*

🔍 **Objective:** Reinforce habit-building and personal accountability.

Activity: Weekly Habit Reflection

📋 **Instructions:**

- Students choose 2–3 habits to track (focus, kindness, prayer).

- Record weekly progress and set new goals.

📱 **Tools:** HabitBull, Google Sheets, Streaks

💡 **Example:**

Naudia tracks "read, pray, smile." On Friday she says, "I missed one prayer day, but I'll start again stronger next week."

📣 Bonus: Tech Leadership Roles in Class

Create rotating student roles that encourage accountability and purpose:

Role	Responsibility
Tech Organizer	Keeps shared devices charged and organized
Focus Timer Captain	Starts the group timer for independent work
Reflection Reporter	Collects daily goals or meditations
Fitness Coach	Leads movement videos or wellness reflections
Digital Encourager	Shares one compliment or scripture weekly via audio

Final Word to Teachers and Program Leaders

You are not competing with the phone.

You are transforming it into a **spiritual and academic ally**.

By using this device with intention, you are:

- Building their confidence

- Shaping their character

- And developing young leaders who will navigate the world—not be consumed by it.

The power within them becomes visible—when their tech reflects who they truly are.

📖 Chapter 11:
Purposeful Tech Use in the Community: Connecting to the Bigger World

"We didn't teach our students to stay small. We trained them to show up—and use their gifts to bless others."

✅ Chapter Purpose:

In this chapter, we guide students, parents, and educators to **bring their purpose-filled phone use into their communities**.

This includes:

- Capturing and reflecting on meaningful moments
- Leading through service and storytelling
- Using devices to amplify truth, hope, growth, and gratitude
- Becoming agents of light in a digital world

🌍 Why Community Integration Matters

Phones shouldn't just be tools for school success or personal development—they should support students in becoming:

- **Witnesses of their own growth**
- **Recorders of goodness**
- **Encouragers to others**
- **Civic-minded creators**
- **Kingdom citizens with a calling**

Let's give our students the tools to take what they've learned and **live it out loud**—in public, in service, and online.

📷 Real-World Activities That Reflect Each Chapter

📖 Chapter 1: Who Am I and What Powers Do I Possess?

Community Activity:

Create a "Power Within Me" community mural or digital slideshow.

📱 Use phones to:

- Take pictures of peers, leaders, or volunteers demonstrating kindness and leadership.

- Add captions like "I see power when…" or "This inspired me because…"

📌 Display during school events, in church lobbies, or on class blogs.

📓 Chapter 2: *Meditation*

Community Activity:

Lead a neighborhood or school-wide "Peace Pause."

📱 Use phones to:

- Play a calming Scripture audio at the start of community meetings

- Teach others how to breathe deeply and focus on peace using their devices

📌 Partner with local youth groups or churches to offer "Meditation & Motivation" booths at events.

📓 Chapter 3: Executive Functioning Skills

Community Activity:

Organize a mini community service project.

📱 Use phones to:

- Assign and track tasks with shared checklists (Google Keep or Trello)

- Set reminders for team roles (trash pickup, welcome station, prayer circle)

📌 Students learn to manage, plan, and complete service with dignity.

📓 Chapter 4: GOP FROG TIME

Community Activity:

Host a "Goal Wall" in a public library or youth center.

📱 Use phones to:

- Record 30-second goal-setting reflections

- Create visual or audio exhibits of student goal journeys

📌 Show others how young people are setting intentions that matter.

📓 Chapter 5: *Reading*

Community Activity:

Start a community "Read & Reflect Club."

📱 Use phones to:

- Record and share book summaries or key lessons via podcast or video

- Invite elders to tell stories and archive them digitally

📌 Bridge generations through digital storytelling.

📕 Chapter 6: *History*

Community Activity:

Document and preserve local history.

📱 Use phones to:

- Interview elders about their experiences growing up

- Record tours of historical landmarks

- Capture cultural celebrations and heritage days

📌 Help students see their roots and their role in continuing the story.

Chapter 7: *Math*

Community Activity:

Organize a "Budget for Blessing" project.

Use phones to:

- Plan a community supply drive or fundraiser

- Track donations and needs in real time using spreadsheet apps

📌 Learn that math isn't just numbers—it's how we bless wisely.

📓 Chapter 8: *Science*

Community Activity:

Start a community "Eco-Explorers" team.

📱 Use phones to:

- Track pollution, water levels, or plant species in the neighborhood

- Record and map environmental improvements (trash cleanups, recycling centers)

📌 Science becomes service—data becomes discipleship.

📔 Chapter 9: Physical Education

Community Activity:

Lead a "Movement for the Mind" event.

📱 Use phones to:

- Record student-led workouts and share as encouragement

- Track step goals or lead "Prayer in Motion" sessions

📌 Connect fitness, joy, and faith in community-based movement.

📓 Chapter 10: *Social Skills*

Community Activity:

Host a "Kindness Audio Booth" at a school or camp.

📱 Use phones to:

- Record messages of hope, gratitude, and encouragement

- Share digital messages of affirmation for classmates, teachers, and staff

📌 Let love speak—digitally and publicly.

📓 Chapter 11: *Good Habits*

Community Activity:

Facilitate a "Habit Challenge" across families or classrooms.

📱 Use phones to:

- Track daily habits like "speak kindly," "pray at lunch," or "read for 10 minutes"

- Share progress through audio check-ins or community dashboards

📌 Teach that good habits build great futures—when we practice them together.

💬 Digital Citizenship In Real Life

Teach students to ask before they post or record:

- Does this reflect who I truly am?
- Does this build someone up?
- Would I want this to represent me years from now?
- Is this how I represent God's voice?

Final Word to the Students

You don't just have a phone—you have a platform.

Use it to:

- Record your growth
- Celebrate your progress
- Teach others what you've learned
- Capture beauty
- Shine light
- Show love
- Leave a legacy

Phones don't define your worth.

You define what your phone reflects.

The power is already in you.

Use it to **bless the world**.

🔖 CLOSING SECTION

📧 A Letter to Parents

Dear Parents,

We understand. Raising children in the digital age feels like walking a tightrope—with love in one hand and responsibility in the other. It's tempting to hide phones, restrict everything, or avoid digital battles altogether. But you know as well as we do:

Avoidance is not training.

Silencing isn't shaping.

And blocking isn't building.

Your child is not only growing a brain—they are forming a worldview. If we don't teach them how to use their phones with wisdom, the world will.

This guide is a partner in your home, a tool for your kitchen table, and a coach at bedtime. Every chapter, every reflection, and every practice was written with love to help your child develop the habits, confidence, and mindset to thrive—not just survive.

Let's stop asking how to control their screen time.

Let's start asking how to use this time to build a life that glorifies God and reflects their purpose.

With deep respect for your role,

– The Unlocking Team

💼 A Letter to Teachers & Summer Program Leaders

Dear Educators and Leaders,

You are not "just teaching."

You are shaping minds, building habits, and awakening purpose.

This curriculum wasn't written to add more to your plate. It was created to **fuel the mission** already on your heart: guiding children toward greatness.

This generation was born into a digital world. That means they don't need less access—they need more guidance. And you are uniquely positioned to provide it.

When students understand how to use phones with intentionality, classrooms become calmer. Confidence grows. Reflection becomes natural. And learning becomes lifelong.

We hope you use this guide not just to teach content—but to **transform how students see themselves** in a noisy, connected world.

With gratitude and partnership,

— The Unlocking Curriculum Team

⚠ Digital Use Disclaimer

This book is intended as an educational and coaching resource. It does not serve as medical advice, therapeutic treatment, or mental health diagnosis. If a student shows signs of emotional distress, compulsive behavior, or digital addiction, please seek help from a licensed professional.

This guide is for empowerment, not evaluation. Use it to create dialogue, build habits, and develop routines that support emotional, spiritual, and academic health.

📝 Sample Agreements for Purposeful Phone Use

Ages 3–5: Modeling and Monitoring

"I will use the phone with my grown-up to learn and grow. We will listen, watch, and reflect together. I will ask before using a phone."

Ages 6–9: Training and Support

"I understand that the phone helps me track good habits, reflect on my goals, and connect with God. I will use it with permission and tell my family how I feel after using it."

Ages 10–13: Reconstruction and Responsibility

"I will use my phone to lead myself, reflect on who I am becoming, and build good habits. I will share my screen time use weekly with my family and stay committed to peace and purpose."

Teenagers: Leadership and Boundaries

"I agree to manage my phone time in a way that reflects my values. I will use my phone to grow, lead, and reflect. I will hold myself accountable to weekly goals, track progress, and talk about challenges when they come."

📖 6-Week Mini-Lesson Plan: Teaching Digital Citizenship

Each lesson is 10–15 minutes and focused on 3 key traits: Wisdom, Respect, and Security.

Week	Focus Topic	Key Questions	Activity
1	What You Post	"Would I say this in person?" "Would I want my grandma or teacher to see this?"	Create a "Digital Mirror" poster: What does your phone say about you?
2	Who Sees It?	"Who follows me?" "What do I allow people to see?"	Review privacy settings. Write down your digital boundaries.
3	Protecting Myself	"What's personal?" "What's unsafe to share?"	Create a digital safety checklist together.
4	What You Reflect	"Do my posts show my values?" "Do I uplift others?"	Choose 1 encouraging thing to share online this week.
5	Integrity Online	"Do I act the same online and offline?"	Role-play online scenarios and write 3 better responses.
6	Digital Legacy	"What do I want to be remembered for online?"	Record a short digital mission statement: "This is who I am becoming."

Additional Resources Toolkit

Recommended Apps & Tools:

Category	Tools
Meditation	Insight Timer, Abide, Soulspace, Headspace for Kids
Habit Tracking	Habitica, HabitBull, Streaks, Google Keep
Voice Journaling	Voice Memos (iOS), Easy Voice Recorder (Android), Flip
Reading & Audio	Epic!, Libby, Audible Kids, Book Creator
Visual Projects	Canva, Adobe Spark, Google Slides, iMovie
Focus & Planning	Forest, Flora, Trello, Google Calendar, Reminders App
Screen Time Monitoring	iPhone Screen Time, Digital Wellbeing (Android)

Scripture for Reflection & Meditation:

- Philippians 4:8
- Jeremiah 29:11
- Romans 12:2
- Proverbs 3:5–6
- Psalm 46:10
- 2 Timothy 1:7

Books & Podcasts for Parents and Educators:

- *Screens and Teens* by Dr. Kathy Koch
- *The Tech-Wise Family* by Andy Crouch
- *Parenting Generation Screen* by Jonathan McKee
- *Raising Emotionally Strong Boys* by David Thomas
- *Brains, Habits & Holy Moments* (Podcast series)

📖 Final Encouragement

"Do not be conformed to the pattern of this world, but be transformed by the renewing of your mind." – Romans 12:2

Your student is a leader.

Your home is a sanctuary.

Your classroom is a launching pad.

And their phone? It's a tool. A mirror. A stage. A planner. A microphone for truth.

Use it to declare the power within.

Thank you for answering the call to lead a generation **not just into the digital age—but into their divine purpose**.

With honor,

– The Unlocking Curriculum Team

🐕 Acknowledgements

This guide would not have been possible without the divine inspiration, daily grace, and unwavering faithfulness of God—who placed this assignment in my heart and provided strength through every stage of its creation.

To the parents who continue to stand in the gap, pray without ceasing, and love with patience and boldness—thank you. Your desire to train up your children in the way they should go is the foundation of generational transformation.

To the teachers, summer program leaders, and educational trailblazers—thank you for seeing every student not as a problem to fix, but as a promise to unlock. You are on the frontlines of shaping minds and nurturing hearts. This guide was written with your challenges and your courage in mind.

To the students who will read, reflect, record, and rise—you are the reason this book exists. The world needs your light, your leadership, and your love for what is good. May you always use your gifts to uplift, not just to scroll. To lead, not just to follow.

To every counselor, youth worker, community partner, and faith-based leader who dares to speak truth, model wisdom, and bring calm into chaos—your work and your witness matter. You are living proof that leadership grounded in love can change lives.

And finally, as the curriculum designer, I would like to acknowledge that during my decade-long tenure as a school administrator, I listened closely to the concerns of teachers, parents, and community members—concerns about the growing, untrained use of digital devices among children and teens. Their heartfelt questions, frustrations, and hopes became the foundation for this guide. This book is not only a response—it is a resource built from those conversations, crafted to serve both the classroom and the home with wisdom and grace.

May this book be used for decades to come as a tool of peace, a voice of truth, and a light for the next generation.

— *The Unlocking Curriculum Team*

✍ Meet the Author

Alisa Ladawn Grace is a retired school administrator, accomplished author, transformational life coach, and visionary curriculum developer with a lifelong passion for empowering others—especially children—to unlock their full spiritual, emotional, and mental potential.

With a **Specialist Degree in Curriculum and Instruction** and decades of experience in educational leadership, Alisa brings a unique blend of academic depth and spiritual insight to every resource she creates. Her work equips individuals of all ages to grow in **clarity, confidence, and Christ-centered character**.

Her writing is both practical and deeply faith-rooted, weaving together **real-life applications, biblical truth, and engaging storytelling** to guide readers toward transformation. Through her children's books and guides, Alisa introduces young minds to the power of the Holy Spirit in everyday decisions. Her most recent release, *I Got the Power: B.A.D. Decision*, empowers children to use their God-given wisdom to make Brain-powered, Actionable, and Disciplined choices.

Other beloved titles include:

- *Powered by the Spirit: A Journey of Kindness and Forgiveness* – a story-driven look at forgiveness through a biblical lens for young readers

- *No Turning Back: Breaking Free from the Grip of Yesterday* – a transformational guide for adults on releasing the past

- *Renewed: The Transformational Power of Putting Off the Old and Putting On the New* – a step-by-step spiritual reset for men and women alike

- *Where Are the Fishers of Men? The Great Commission: Lost in the Crowd!* – a compelling challenge to revive the mission of discipleship in modern faith communities

Her latest curriculum-based work, *Unlocking Your Great Potential Within You: The Supernatural Powers of Meditation, Executive Functioning Skills, and Good Habits*, reflects her deep calling to shape the next generation through **faith-driven practices and purposeful tech use**. This guide equips parents, teachers, summer program leaders, and students with the tools to build calm, focus, and character in a fast-paced, distracted world.

Whether she's ministering through a training, a children's story, or a leadership seminar, **Alisa's voice is one of grace, wisdom, and unwavering hope**. Her life's mission is simple yet powerful: to help people of all ages know who they are, why they're here, and how to walk in their God-given potential every single day.

Unlocking Your Great Potential Within You
The Supernatural Powers of Meditation, Executive Functioning Skills, and Good Habits
A Guide for Raising Purposeful and Powerful Digital Citizens

In today's fast-paced, tech-driven world, children are being handed powerful devices before they're equipped with powerful habits. This transformational guide is designed to help parents, teachers, and youth leaders reclaim the digital space—not by restriction alone, but through faith-filled training, intentional strategies, and guided reflection.

Blending biblical truth with practical tools, Unlocking Your Great Potential Within You introduces children to the supernatural powers they already carry: the peace of meditation, the clarity of executive functioning skills, and the structure of good habits. Through stories, interactive lessons, family activities, classroom implementation strategies, and real-life applications, this guide empowers the next generation to:

Cultivate calm in a noisy world

Lead themselves with purpose and accountability

Develop digital habits that reflect their God-given identity

Strengthen communication, kindness, and character

Build consistent routines at home, in school, and in the community

Whether you're a parent, teacher, or mentor, this guide provides everything you need to raise wise, reflective, and resilient children who use their phones—and their lives—with purpose.

It's not just about limiting screen time.
It's about unlocking what's already within.

www.ingramcontent.com/pod-product-compliance
Lightning Source LLC
Chambersburg PA
CBHW080544090426

42734CB00016B/3197